Beetles

By Edana Eckart

Children's Press®
A Division of Scholastic Inc.
New York / Toronto / London / Auckland / Sydney
Mexico City / New Delhi / Hong Kong
Danbury, Connecticut

Photo Credits: Cover © Michael & Patricia Fogden/Corbis; p. 5 © Earl & Nazima Kowall/Corbis; p. 7 © Doug Wechsler/Nature Picture Library; pp. 9, 15 © Geoff Dore/Nature Picture Library; p. 11 © Premaphotos/Nature Picture Library; p. 13 © Bruce Davidson/Nature Picture Library; p. 17 © Ralph A. Clevenger/Corbis; p. 19 © Dietmar Nill/Nature Picture Library; p. 21 © ChiselVision/Corbis
Contributing Editor: Jennifer Silate
Book Design: Mindy Liu

Library of Congress Cataloging-in-Publication Data

Eckart, Edana.
   Beetles / by Edana Eckart.
   v. cm.—(Animals of the world)
   Contents: Beetles—Wings—Different colors.
   ISBN 0-516-24300-4 (lib. bdg.)—ISBN 0-516-27880-0 (pbk.)
   1. Beetles—Juvenile literature. [1. Beetles.] I. Title. II: Series:
Eckart, Edana. Animals of the world.

QL576.2.E35 2003
595.76—dc21

                                        2002155463

Contents

A **beetle** is an **insect**.

There are many kinds of beetles.

Beetles live almost everywhere in the world.

Most beetles live on land.

Some beetles live in the water.

Beetles have **wings**.

Most beetles can fly.

Some beetles are very large.

The largest beetle in the world is a **Goliath beetle**.

Beetles eat many things.

Many beetles eat plants.

15

Beetles are many colors.

Ladybugs are red with black spots.

Some beetles **glow** in the dark.

Fireflies glow in the dark.

19

Beetles are interesting insects.

21

New Words

beetle (**beet**-l) an insect with hard wings that cover a pair of soft wings used to fly

fireflies (**fire**-fliez) small beetles that fly at night and glow in the dark

glow (**gloh**) to give off a steady, low light

Goliath beetle (guh-**lye**-uhth-**beet**-l) the largest beetle in the world

insect (**in**-sekt) a kind of animal that is very small and has three pairs of legs

ladybugs (**lay**-dee-buhgz) small, round beetles that usually have red or orange wings and black spots

wings (**wingz**) the parts of the body that an animal uses to fly

To Find Out More

Books

Beetles
by Sandra Donovan
Raintree Publishers

Bugs, Beetles, and Butterflies
by Harry Ziefert
Viking Penguin

Web Site
Enchanted Learning: Beetles
http://www.enchantedlearning.com/subjects/insects/
    beetles/printouts.shtml
Learn about many different kinds of beetles on this Web site.

Index

About the Author

Edana Eckart has written several children's books. She enjoys bike riding with her family.

Reading Consultants

Kris Flynn, Coordinator, Small School District Literacy, The San Diego County Office of Education

Shelly Forys, Certified Reading Recovery Specialist, W.J. Zahnow Elementary School, Waterloo, IL

Sue McAdams, Former President of the North Texas Reading Council of the IRA, and Early Literacy Consultant, Dallas, TX